The Church You'v Longed For

What You Can Do To Make It Happen

Adult Journal

Dedicated to David Jones and our friends at Scripture Union, whose longings for the church parallel ours.

Contents

Reach us on the Internet: http://www.reapernet.com

This journal was created with input from more than 40 pastors and laypersons from across North America.

Writing team: David R. Mains, Director; Patric Knaak, Laurie Mains, Marian Oliver, Randy Petersen, Mitchell Vander Vorst

Editors: Marian Oliver and Mitchell Vander Vorst
Cover Illustration: Joe VanSeveren
Cover Design: Bethany Hissong
Text Design: Blum Graphic Design

The Chapel Ministries is a nonprofit, nondenominational, international Christian outreach dedicated to helping God's church grow spiritually and numerically by revitalizing its members, whether they be gathered or scattered, to be a force for kingdom purposes worldwide. To support this goal, The Chapel Ministries provides print and media resources including the annual 50-Day Spiritual Adventure and the 4-Week Worship Celebration, the daily half-hour television program "You Need to Know," and seasonal radio programming. Year-round Bible study guides are offered through a Joint Ministry Venture with Scripture Union U.S.A., to encourage the healthy spiritual habits of daily Scripture reading and prayer.

Printed in the United States of America

ISBN 1-57849-000-6

Introduction

What do you want your church to be?

Friendly? Growing? Worshipful?

Maybe your church is already all you could ever want. If so, you are blessed. But chances are, there are still some areas of frustration. You dream of what the church can be, and you don't understand why it's not.

You long for a place that accepts you fully, a place where you truly belong. You desire the care and support that comes from a group of believers who put others first and practice the compassion of Christ. You want your church to clear out its secrets and start dealing honestly and lovingly with a needy world.

Our hopes get dashed on one "minor" drawback: The church is full of people—faulty, fallible people—who often keep things from working the way they should.

Maybe you're not in a church, and that's *because* of all those faulty, fallible people. You have an idea of what a church should be, but you haven't found a place that matches up.

If only the church would wake up, support and strengthen its members, learn to care for the community, get rid of petty hypocrisies, and boldly act with the heart of Jesus Christ. Yeah, if only that could happen.

Well, it can. After all, who is really in charge here? God, who breathes new life into dry bones, who forgives sins and heals diseases, who puts his love in our hearts. When God gets hold of a church, miracles happen. Oh, people are still faulty and fallible, and there will always be some problems. But God can transform the worst of situations into the church you've always longed for. And you can play a key role.

You see, it's easy to say, "They ought to get their act together," but you're a part of that act! What can you do to be more caring, more inviting, more honest? The action steps in this Adventure help you make individual changes that in turn will transform your church into a better place. And if your church is a great place already, these steps will help ensure that it stays that way.

We have identified eight major characteristics of thriving churches. There are more, but these are the themes we're focusing on.

The church you've always longed for . . .

- Works at being a caring family.
- Captures the heart of the community.
- Welcomes all people.
- Empowers each individual.
- Models integrity.
- Serves a broken world.
- Encounters the living God.
- Anticipates a great future.

We'll be exploring these eight themes throughout this journal.

We hope your church is going on this Adventure together. The combined life-changes of a whole congregation should have great impact on a church. But even if you are going solo, this Adventure should make you a better church member, and you just might begin to affect others around you. If you're not presently involved in a church, why not seek out a congregation that's doing the Adventure? (You can call 1-800-224-2735 for suggestions.) Maybe you'll find a good connection.

In any case, we trust that God will use this Adventure to revolutionize your church involvement.

THE FOURTH STREET CHURCH WAS DESPERATELY
IN NEED OF A MASTER PLAN.

What People Are Saying About the 50-Day Adventure

he 50-Day Adventure has made me more aware of God's being in total control over erything. . . . It has also brought my wife and me closer, as well as people in our urch."   —Jack N., Michigan

his Adventure has really helped me focus on God's Word. Sometimes we all get busy d forget our priorities. This study has certainly helped us get our priorities in the right der. This is the third year we have done the Adventure. I look forward to each one."
—Marianne L., Maryland

Iy wife was continually trying to get me to be more active and to have a personal rela- nship with Christ. I did not know what that was. I went to a small group with her and rted doing the 50-Day Adventure. I started to spend time with the Lord and prayed for deep and earnest desire to seek him and know his Word. He answered my prayers and w I seek him daily. . . . I spent 40 years avoiding him and now I want to spend every inute with him. Thank you!"   —David H., Colorado

felt a sense of unity knowing that during the Adventure most people in my church re studying the very same lessons. . . . Also, I really liked having my kids involved with sons that were appropriate for them."   —Janie S., Kentucky

am an inmate. My cellie and I worked together in the Adventure journal and we ve grown spiritually. . . . God has blessed me and shown me I have a lot to be thank- for, even here in prison."   —Mark D., Pennsylvania

Jur small group was floundering. We would gather on Wednesday nights to fellow- ip and pray, but we lacked direction and purpose. The first meeting after starting the -Day Spiritual Adventure was filled with excitement! Our group was infused with w life and a fresh desire to seek the Lord!"   —Becky H., Colorado

he Adventure taught me to dedicate time to God each day. I have a six-year-old ughter, so the only time I could do the Adventure uninterrupted was early in the orning. After doing this for 50 days, it's a great habit!"   —Chris B., Colorado

How Should I Use This Journal?

This is more than an ordinary booklet you're holding. It's a guide for accelerated spiritual growth. It's a road map to lead you on an Adventure that can change your life. Two months from now, as you've allowed God's Spirit to work, you will be different—a stronger Christian in a renewed relationship with your church.

More than 650,000 people are on this Spiritual Adventure with you. Thousands of churches will benefit as the Lord touches individual lives. And all of that starts as you turn these pages and begin to study the Scriptures, pray, and put into practice the action steps in this journal. There's a lot going on here, but don't be overwhelmed. Just take the Adventure step by step and you'll be fine.

▪ What do I need?

1. Your Bible. Each day we offer a passage of Scripture for you to read, along with a few questions to help you get at the meaning of the text and how it applies to the Adventure. Make sure you're using a Bible you feel comfortable with and can understand.

2. This journal. Here is where you'll be processing what's going on in your life. The journal has instructions for each day. Don't lose it.

3. The Adventure Guidebook—*I Like Church, But . . .* by Dan Lupton. This essential book will help you understand the themes of the Adventure, giving you the big picture of the changes you (and perhaps your church) are making. Read a chapter a week to keep current (reading time: maybe half an hour per chapter). Contact your church, your local Christian bookstore, or The Chapel Ministries for your copy (see p. 21).

4. A good attitude. This Adventure will stretch you. Take it seriously, but not too seriously. Have fun with it, but let God's Spirit work within you to make some important changes.

▪ What do I need to do?

There are assignments for you to complete each day of the Adventure. First, you'll need to read the assigned Scripture passage in your Bible and answer the questions in the journal. Scripture reading is an important part of this Adventure and one of the healthy spiritual habits we hope you will take away with you after these 50 days. And if you're up for an extra challenge, we recommend that you choose some Bible verses to memorize. Pick the ones most meaningful to you. The *Make It Happen Scripture Pack* is a helpful resource with 15 Adventure-related verses.

Second, you will need to read a chapter every week in the Adventure Guidebook.

Dan Lupton. This book will lead you through the Adventure with helpful insights and in-depth explanations of each theme. It also provides extra ideas on how to make the Adventure "real" for you. And then there are the action steps. . . .

What are these "action steps"?

They're specific activities we're suggesting to help you apply the Adventure themes. The next few pages will explain the steps thoroughly. The first action step is a daily prayer. That's easy enough, but it sets the tone for everything else in the Adventure.

The second action step involves saying positive things about your church. The third involves getting to know someone outside your usual circle. The fourth is a matter of encouraging someone in a very practical way. In the fifth step, we challenge you to "take out" some "garbage" in your life.

The Adventure works well when you follow our suggestions, but you may choose to tailor the steps to fit your situation. If one of the steps is driving you crazy, forget it and focus on the others. Better to have four important life changes than five noble attempts cut short by a nervous breakdown! Or if you can handle more, do it! (For a quick preview of all the Adventure assignments, see p. 9.)

How much of a time commitment is involved here?

We estimate that it will take just 10 to 15 minutes per day, with a few extra time blocks strewn throughout the 50-day period for completion of some action steps.

On a typical day, you will be given Scripture to read and questions to help you grapple with it. You'll be reminded to pray the daily prayer. Then we may prompt you to read a chapter of the Adventure Guidebook or to do specific action steps.

How do I keep track of all the stuff I need to do?

We will prompt you throughout this journal to keep current with the action steps. For a quick overview of where you've been and where you're headed each week, see the "Looking Back . . . Moving Forward" pages, usually after each Friday journal page. Still, it might be helpful to map out the Adventure at the start. As you look over the next few pages, put some notes on your personal calendar about the big things you'll be doing.

Do I need to follow the journal every day?

Yes. But if you miss a day or two, keep going. It's best to pick up the journal entries with the current day, rather than try to make up for lost time.

- **What's special about Saturday/Sunday pages?**
  Each of the eight themes is introduced with a format that is different from the oth
  journal pages. It includes a commentary by Dr. David Mains.

- **Can I do the Adventure with my friends or family?**
  Absolutely. That's a great way to make it even more meaningful. This will take some ext
  time as you discuss the Scriptures or review one another's progress on the action steps, b
  the mutual encouragement and accountability will be a great blessing. And we provi
  lots of help with age-graded journals for families and small group materials for adults. F
  specific ideas, get the pamphlet *Adventuring with Friends and Family* from your church
  call The Chapel Ministries at 1-800-224-2735.

- **What if I want an extra challenge?**
  We've suggested additional resources to help you customize the Adventure to me
  your needs. On each "Looking Back . . . Moving Forward" page, you'll find option
  follow-up scriptures and a recommended book for further study. We've reviewe
  dozens of titles and believe these are the best available on the Adventure themes.

- **What can I do to keep going when the Adventure is over?**
  Once you've finished the Adventure you may want to continue with some of the spir
  tual habits you've developed over these 50 days. On page 76 we have a great idea t
  help you keep going. Take 30 seconds now to turn to page 76 and look it over.

- **Don't you have the Adventure on TV and radio?**
  You bet. "You Need to Know," an award-winning talk show hosted by David Main
  airs on many Christian TV stations across the country. In the spring and summer
  1997, the program will cover the themes of this Adventure. Numerous radio statior
  will be playing the two-minute "Adventure Highlight." To find out where to tune i
  call The Chapel Ministries at 1-800-224-2735.

- **Where should I start?**
  Familiarize yourself with the five action steps on pages 10–18. It will also be helpful
  flip through the day-to-day section of the journal starting on page 22. This way yo
  will have an idea of what will be coming. Then, to give yourself a head start, begin tr
  Warm-up Day exercises on the Friday before Day 1 of the Adventure (p. 19).

Assignment Preview

Read this summary to get acquainted with the Adventure and to see how often the various assignments and action steps are to be done. (For a full description of the action steps, see pp. 10–18.) Remember: This journal will give you daily reminders and weekly checkups to guide you through the assignments.

DAILY

Study the assigned Scripture passages and answer the questions in the journal.

Pray the Listening with Jesus Prayer using the model on page 11.

Write down something you appreciate about your church or people in your church. Use the chart on pages 40–41.

TWICE EACH WEEK

Tell someone else what you appreciate about your church.

WEEKLY

Read the appropriate chapter in *I Like Church, But . . .* by Dan Lupton (see p. 21).

ONCE DURING THE ADVENTURE

Get together with a person outside your normal circle of friends (see p. 13).

Empower someone by helping him or her develop an interest or ability (see p. 15).

Throw away some "trash" from your life (see p. 17).

Invite someone to church.

Action Step 1
Learn to Listen with the Ears of Jesus

The exasperated dad scolds his nine-year-old girl. "I've been calling you for five minutes to come downstairs for dinner!"

"Sorry, Dad," she answers. "I didn't hear you."

The truth is, he was calling loud enough, but she wasn't listening. Her mind was on her video game.

The wife is frustrated with her husband. "But I told you about this party last Monday!"

"You did not!"

"I did! You were sitting right here watching the game."

"Well, there you have it," the husband quips. "How do you expect me to hear you when I'm watching a game?"

The words entered his ears, but not his mind. He wasn't listening.

If you long for your church to be more of a caring family, you need to become a more caring family member. Believe it or not, one way to do that is to change the way you *hear*.

As you read the gospels, one thing becomes apparent—Jesus had great ears. He was always picking up the cries of those around him. He had a kind of radar for human need. He didn't just hear, he listened.

As Jesus' disciples, we are to show his kind of love to one another within the church and to others outside the church (John 13:35; Galatians 6:10). Many of us have hearts that overflow with compassion when we become aware of people's suffering, but we aren't always good at *becoming* aware. We may have Jesus' heart, but we need his ears.

Think about a typical day at church. Do you walk right past people with deep needs? You may smile and shake hands but miss the urgent message under the surface: "SOS! I need some care!"

Think about a typical day at work, or just driving around the community or talking with friends. People around you may be crying out for someone to love them, to really love them with Jesus' kind of love, but are you hearing those cries? Are you listening with Jesus' ears?

The kind of church you've always longed for is a caring family, one that works hard to be attentive to needs within the church and without. You can do your part by tuning in to Jesus' frequency, trusting him to train your ears to hear as he does.

Directions: Every day of the Adventure, say the Listening with Jesus Prayer. Feel free to put it in your own words, but try to keep the basic idea. You're asking the Lord for guidance and checking in to see if you are hearing the same things he's hearing. This is the sort of prayer that will affect your whole life. You will begin hearing everything in a new way.

Tip: You might develop a catchphrase that you can remember and repeat throughout the day: "Let me hear with your ears, Lord," or just "Ears of compassion, Lord." Send these sentence prayers to God from time to time each day.

The Listening with Jesus Prayer

Lord,

I long to be part of a caring church family,

But often I'm not sensitive to what

   people are really saying.

Please teach me to listen with your

   ears of compassion.

I pray for _____.
                    [a need you've heard recently]

Lord, help me respond with a heart that

   cares the way you do.

Amen.

11

Action Step 2
Attract Others by Saying Good Things About the Church

Once upon a time, there was a woman named Ethel who went to church every week. And every week she was frustrated because her pastor refused to give an invitation at the end of the service. Ethel felt it was important to invite people to walk forward and accept Christ, but the pastor wouldn't do it.

Every Monday at work, her longtime friend Harriet asked about her weekend. And every Monday Ethel complained about that hardheaded pastor of hers. "He wouldn't know a good idea if it socked him in the face," she muttered.

One week, Ethel suggested for the zillionth time that the pastor give an invitation. "Hmmm," he said, "that might be a good idea." Ethel was shocked. "If you get someone who needs the Lord to church, then I will offer an invitation."

Ethel couldn't wait for Monday to roll around. She marched up to her friend Harriet. "Would you come to church with me this week?"

"No," said Harriet, with a quizzical look.

"But you're my oldest and dearest friend," Ethel blurted. "Why not?"

"Well, I'd do just about anything for you, Ethel," replied Harriet. "But for two years I've been hearing what an imbecile your pastor is—I'll never, ever go there."

We Christians can be expert complainers. We carp about every little detail of church life and then wonder why people don't want to come. We may long for our church to capture the heart of our community, we may yearn for our church to have a good reputation—but how can it when we're always complaining about what's wrong?

What if we changed our strategy by changing our attitude? What if we started focusing on the good things about our churches (Philippians 4:8)? What if we regularly told others, inside the church and out, about those good things? What if each church member became sort of a public relations rep for the church? We might just give people reasons for wanting to come, rather than reasons for staying away.

Directions: (Part 1) Every day write down something good about your church (or people in your church family) on pages 40–41. It should be fun to see how many things you can come up with. Then, at least twice each week, tell someone about one of those good things. You can share with fellow parishioners, but each week try to talk to at least one person outside your church.

(Part 2) Also, once during the Adventure, invite someone to your church. Once you've been saying good things about the church for a while, people will want to come. (If you're doing this Adventure in the spring, Easter would be a great time to invite people.)

Action Step 3
Connect with Individuals Outside Your Circle

You know what the hottest trend is these days in TV sitcoms? Groups of friends. In most cases the concept is simple: A circle of friends about the same age, with similar interests, living in the same area—well, these people get together and, well, they talk, and they joke around, and they have fun because they're, like, friends.

And these shows can be funny, for about a half hour. But if you had to live with these characters, it would get old fast.

Some churches are like that. Everybody's alike. Within the circle, everyone is comfortable; they've grown accustomed to each other. But there are few surprises anymore—they know each other too well. And if an outsider who doesn't fit the mold shows up , he or she quickly realizes, "I don't belong here."

"Cheers." Now that was a sitcom with a difference. A psychologist mingled with a letter carrier; an ex-ballplayer hung out with a grad student. Granted, a bar is not the healthiest place to while away the hours, but that place had something many churches lack. No matter who walked in that door, the person was greeted enthusiastically—whatever his status or income or occupation.

Do you long for that kind of church, one that warmly welcomes people of different races, classes, ages, and backgrounds? Do you want your church to be characterized by outgoing friendliness and acceptance? Well, that attitude needs to start with you.

How warmly do you welcome people who differ from you in race, class, age, or other ways? Not just in church, but in your whole life. How broad is your circle of friends? Do you feel comfortable with different kinds of people?

We need to reach out of our personal circles of comfort, making it a point to get to know people who are not like us. In so doing, we will broaden our own horizons, breaking barriers, learning to understand and accept those of different backgrounds. When a church is full of people who regularly reach out like this, it can finally become a place where "everybody knows your name."

Directions: (Part 1) Start by evaluating the circle of friends and associates you have now. This may pinpoint some ways in which you could enlarge your circle. Consider areas such as age, race, religion, economics, education, or marital and family status.

(Part 2) After your analysis, it's time to take a step. Select a person who is outside your normal circle of friends. This may be someone you vaguely know at work or church or in the neighborhood, or just someone you pass every day without really knowing him or her at all. If you would like to select two people, the benefit to you will be that much greater.

(Part 3) Then, find a way to get to know this person. Arrange to go out for lunch or coffee, or brunch after church. Go bowling or miniature golfing, or arrange to attend a concert or play together. Take a kid to a baseball game. Remember, your purpose is simply to get to know someone new. You will enlarge your world, but don't give the impression that this is just a "learning experience" for you. Relax. Be a friend. Here are some tips and questions that will help you plan this action step.

Tips for Connecting with Individuals Outside Your Circle

Helpful hints: Be careful about male-female relationships. Avoid date-like situations that might cause misunderstanding. Married couples may want to do this step together. In the case of an unbeliever, be wise about your evangelistic efforts. Naturally your faith will spill out as you express yourself, but be courteous.

Here are some questions to get you started.
1. Do you have a family? Tell me about them.
2. What was your childhood like? Where did you grow up? Brothers? Sisters?
3. How did you get into your present line of work?
4. What do you like to do when you're not at work?
5. What's the best thing that's happened to you in the last year?
6. What personal dream do you hope will come true someday?
7. *(for a friend from church)* What brought you to this church?
8. *(for a friend from church)* How did you become a Christian?

This action step is completed when you have met with the person you have chosen, but we hope you discover a friendship here that you'll want to continue on your own.

Action Step 4
Help Each Other Become All God Wants Us to Be

Diamonds don't come out of the ground polished and perfect. Many are till "in the rough." It takes a keen eye to notice them and hard work to make them parkle, but the results make up for all the effort.

The church needs more "diamond prospectors," believers who will see one another for who they can become in Christ. Don't you long for a congregation that empowers individuals to live up to the full potential God has for them? We need Christians who will look for ways to invest their efforts, their encouragement, and perhaps even some money to give others a chance to serve God with their talents.

Think about someone who empowered you. Was there a teacher, a coach, a youth director, or a friend who encouraged you to go further than you would have gone on your own? Was there anyone who went beyond the kind words, who actually taught you a craft, gave you a job, put you on a committee, lent you some start-up money?

Remember the biblical example of Barnabas, "The Encourager." Not only did he believe in the self-starter Saul (Paul), but he commended him to the apostles so his ministry could expand. Barnabas also believed in John Mark, a slow starter who had failed in the past but who ended up an associate of Peter and author of the Gospel of Mark. The church through the ages has been blessed not just by the encouraging words of Barnabas, but by his empowering actions.

Directions: Look at the people around you in a new way. Everybody has some interest or skill that isn't fully developed. Notice areas of potential in individuals you encounter at church, at work, or in your neighborhood. Pray about your observations, and then take a step to help one person become all God wants him or her to be. You might say:

"I love to sit in front of you in church. You sing hymns very well. You ought to consider being in the choir."

"You obviously have a gift for hospitality. If a few of us come over one night, will you show us your secrets?"

Or, you might comment to a teen:

"I've noticed your interest in sound systems. How would you like to help me in the sound room? I'll teach you everything I know."

As you talk, make sure you both feel comfortable. Don't turn this into a control situation. The idea is that believers empower each other. One way you can do that for someone is to follow your "ABCs." You might play one of three roles:

Agent. For actors and writers, an agent is someone who guides them in the right direction. The agent not only offers career advice, but calls up potential employers, too. You may need to act as an "agent" for someone by finding ways the person can develop and use his or her talents. In the church, call the chair of a committee that could include this person. In the business world, make contacts for the person. Don't just suggest an educational institution; get the catalog. Don't just mention the summer mission trip; call the coordinator.

Banker. Many people stop short of realizing their dreams because they don't have the money for school, or they lack the capital for some equipment they need. Could you invest some money to bankroll the development of another person? If God has blessed you with more than you need, why not consider using some of it to help someone take crucial steps? Can you pay tuition? Can you buy equipment?

Coach. Maybe you have a special skill you'd like to pass on. It might be woodworking or gardening or teaching Sunday school or quilting. Wouldn't it be great to find someone with a similar interest and offer to teach that person what you know? You could have a wonderful time serving as a mentor.

NO, NO, NO, KIDS. THE SONG IS CALLED "SACRIFICE OF PRAISE,"
NOT "SACKS OF RICE ON TRAYS."

Action Step 5
Get Rid of Personal Garbage That Pollutes God's Church

Several years ago, New York City had a crippling labor strike. What essential workers were involved? Air traffic controllers? Police? Firefighters? Teachers? Nope. Garbage collectors. Trash bags sat on curbs for weeks. Dumpsters overflowed. Rats had a field day. The whole city smelled to high heaven.

Sad to say, the church often suffers from poor garbage disposal. No, this has nothing to do with cleaning up after a potluck supper. It has to do with cleaning up our lives on a regular basis.

Do you long for the church to be a model of integrity? Do you ache from the scandals that have plagued too many churches and ministries? Do you want the church to be honest and clean and whole?

The church's integrity starts with our own. Each of us has garbage, stuff God isn't pleased with. Instead of confessing it and getting rid of it, we let it sit. While we should be regularly taking out the trash, we usually just work at ignoring it. We may get used to the foul aroma, but visitors can usually smell it a mile away.

What "garbage" are you allowing to pile up in your life? We're not just talking about things other people can see. Hidden sins cause real problems in the church as well. On a physical level, what objects are in your home or office that foul up your life? We tend to think of the more obvious sins and their paraphernalia, such as pornography or occult involvement. Certainly materials associated with these sins have no place in your life. But what objects tend to keep you from fully following Christ?

What sort of entertainment do you allow to enter your mind (TV shows, movies, etc.)? Are there certain "socially acceptable" magazines, videos, or CDs that still fill your mind with bad thoughts? Are there tabloid newspapers, lottery tickets, or potato chips that inhibit the kind of wholeness God wants for you? If so, get rid of this stuff. Take the TV guide or videos or magazines and literally put them in the trash.

Why toss this stuff? For one thing, such objects can be a continuing source of temptation. But there's more than that. By discarding these "idols," we are reaffirming our devotion to the one true God. We are signaling that we want nothing to get between us and our great Lord. "Put to death," Paul writes, "whatever belongs to your earthly nature: sexual immorality, impurity, lust, evil desires and greed, which is idolatry." We toss these things so we can "put on the new self, which is being renewed in knowledge in the image of its Creator" (Colossians 3:5,10).

But let's not stop with the physical artifacts. There are other sins fouling up our lives that don't have such a physical presence. Gossip, greed, grudges, complaining, jealousy, dishonesty. You need to take out this trash, too. Maybe you could toss some symbolic object representing the spiritual garbage you are discarding.

Of course, it's the Lord who actually takes out our spiritual trash. Jesus' blood cleanses us from sin, but he asks us to turn away from those misdeeds, to repent. Then the sweet aroma of Christ's presence will fill our lives.

And then maybe your church will be a breath of fresh air.

Directions: Once during the Adventure, evaluate those behaviors, involvements, or attitudes that are polluting your life and God's church. Ask the Holy Spirit to help you identify these things.

If there are physical objects associated with these sins—books, videos, clothing, and so on—take a trash bag and throw them away.

If there are no physical objects directly involved with these sins, see if you can find a symbolic object. If your main hindrance is pride or vanity, throw out a picture of yourself or a mirror. If it's greed, throw away a voided check.

If you can't think of a symbolic object, simply write down the behavior that is polluting your life. Then take the paper and destroy it in some way.

Whatever method you choose, make it an act of worship, renouncing these hindrances in order to follow Christ more fully.

YOU SAID WHAT I SHARED IN COUNSEL WAS CONFIDENTIAL
AND **THEN** WHAT DID YOU PREACH ON? . . . SIN!

The Church You've
Always Longed For

Read Ephesians 3:14–21.

Date _____

1. According to verse 21, where is God's glory to be manifested?

_____

_____

2. What are some of Paul's longings for the church in Ephesus as expressed in these verses? _____

_____

_____

_____

3. Of the prayer requests Paul made for the Ephesian church, which do you long for most? Why? _____

_____

_____

4. When in your church experience have you come close to realizing Paul's aspirations? _____

_____

5. Reread verses 20–21. Do you believe God has the same power to work in the church today? Explain. _____

_____

_____

■ ■

☐ **read** the introductory material on pages 3–9.

☐ **pray** the Listening with Jesus Prayer on page 11.

☐ **read** the introduction in *I Like Church, But* . . . (see p. 21).

The Church You've Always Longed For

Read 1 Peter 2:9–12.

Date _____

1. List the ways Peter refers to the church in this passage. Which of these titles is most meaningful for you? Why? _____

_____

2. According to Peter, how should believers live in a manner consistent with their titles? _____

_____

3. Has there ever been a time when your attitude toward a group was soured because one member's actions left a "bad taste in your mouth"? In what ways does that experience relate to Peter's words in this passage?

_____

_____

_____

4. Describe a time when someone left you with a "good taste" for the church.

_____

_____

5. Peter says, "Once you were not a people, but now you are the people of God." As you anticipate this 50-Day Adventure, what do you long to see happen among God's people in your church? _____

_____

_____

■ ■

☐ **read** the action step descriptions on pages 10–18.

☐ **pray** the Listening with Jesus Prayer on page 11.

☐ **read** the introduction in *I Like Church, But . . .* (see p. 21).

Looking Back

Check the box if you have completed the assignment.

☐ Read the introductory material on pages 3–18.
☐ Read the introduction in the *I Like Church, But . . .* Guidebook.
☐ Completed the Warm-up Days on pages 19–20.

Theme 1:
Work at caring for your church family

Moving forward

Assignments for This Week:

☐ Read chapter 1 in the *I Like Church, But . . .* Guidebook.
☐ Tell two people what you appreciate about your church (see p. 12).

Daily Assignments:

☐ Read the assigned Scripture passages and answer the questions.
☐ Pray the Listening with Jesus Prayer (see p. 11).
☐ Write down something you appreciate about your church (pp. 40–41).

Necessary Resources for This 50-Day Adventure:

I Like Church, But . . . by Dan Lupton (Adventure Guidebook or Audio Guidebook)

In addition to your journals, each household needs one copy of the Adventure Guidebook. This essential, easy-to-read book includes a chapter for each of the eight Adventure themes. In it you'll find:

- Motivational Adventure insights and inspiration.
- Practical helps and illustrations.
- In-depth Adventure theme explanations.
- Additional action step suggestions.

We also recommend the *Make It Happen Scripture Pack.* It includes the Listening with Jesus Prayer and 15 verses related to the Adventure themes. You'll find this pack extremely helpful for memorizing Scripture to undergird your Adventure experience.

Request your copies of these resources today. Use the order form on page 80 in this journal for convenient home delivery, or ask for these resources at your church or local Christian bookstore.

Day 1

Sunday, Date _____

Theme 1 runs Sunday through Friday, Days 1–6.

 Pray

Lord, you modeled what caring for others looks like. Help me, as a part of your church, to keep that tradition alive.

 Read

Read Acts 2:42–47 and 4:32–35.

 Reflect

If a restaurant gives the impression it doesn't care about its patrons, it's going to be in trouble before long. Even years of quality service can be quickly undermined by carelessness in this area. What's true about food is even more critical for places where "spiritual food" is served.

Becoming a caring church is not something that's resolved by agreeing, "This is a good idea; let's come up with a clever logo." Everybody needs to own the concept and work at making it a reality. Even then, it takes time to build the kind of reputation for caring we desire. But, oh, the excitement when word gets around that "here you'll find the extended family you always wanted to be part of."

That's what these two passages reveal about the New Testament church. And it's what a congregation needs to be today to live up to the billing "The Church You've Always Longed For."

 Apply

As you read these passages, what seems especially attractive to you about the early church?

_____

_____

Picture your church members caring for one another as these early believers did. In what ways do you see yourself meeting the needs of others?

_____

_____

_____

 Pray

Pray the Listening with Jesus Prayer.

theme 1:
Work at Caring for
Your Church Family

day 2

Monday

Date _____

Read Mark 10:46–52.

1. This miracle happened as Jesus was on his way to Jerusalem to face his crucifixion. What in this passage shows that he remained sensitive to the needs of others?

_____

2. In Jesus' day blind people were socially powerless. Who are socially powerless people today to whom your church might reach out?

_____

_____

3. Action Step 1 is "Learn to Listen with the Ears of Jesus." In what specific ways could you become more sensitive to the needs of others?

_____

_____

_____

4. The Listening with Jesus Prayer (p. 11) gives you the chance to pray for a need you've heard recently. What need could you fill in today?

_____

_____

■ ■

☐ **pray** the Listening with Jesus Prayer on page 11.

☐ **Write** down something you appreciate about your church on page 40.

☐ **read** chapter 1 in *I Like Church, But* . . . this week (see p. 21).

theme 1:
Work at Caring for
Your Church Family

Date _____

Read Romans 12:9–16.

1. Which of Paul's instructions does your church follow well? If possible, give an example. _____

_____

_____

2. Which commands do you long to see your church practice more?

_____

_____

_____

3. What is one area where you need to improve to help your church become a more caring family? _____

_____

4. Have you had someone rejoice or mourn with you recently? How did that make you feel? How good are you at doing that for others? Explain.

_____

_____

_____

_____

☐ **pray** the Listening with Jesus Prayer on page 11.

☐ **Write** down something you appreciate about your church on page 40.

☐ **tell** someone what you appreciate about your church (see p. 12).

theme 1:
Work at Caring for
Your Church Family

day 4

Wednesday

Date _____

Read 1 John 4:7–12.

1. In one sentence, summarize what John is saying.

_____

_____

_____

2. List some of the reasons John gives to encourage us to love one another. How can reminding yourself of these reasons help you care for people who seem unlovable?

_____

_____

_____

3. Would a visitor to church be able to recognize that love is important to your congregation? Why? _____

_____

_____

4. What keeps you from loving people as you long to do? What is one barrier to caring for others that you would like to overcome during this Adventure?

_____

"One wise person suggested that we take a tip from nature: our ears aren't made to shut, but our mouths are. . . . Listening may be all the caring needed." Dan Lupton, *I Like Church, But . . .*, page 18

◾ ◾

☐ **pray** the Listening with Jesus Prayer on page 11.

☐ **Write** down something you appreciate about your church on page 40.

☐ **read** chapter 1 in *I Like Church, But . . .* this week (see p. 21).

theme 1:
Work at Caring for
Your Church Family

Read 2 Samuel 9:1–13.

1. David had an extremely close relationship with Jonathan and had promised always to be kind to Jonathan's family (see 1 Samuel 20:12–17). What in today's passage shows that David followed through in caring for others?

_____

_____

2. How would you describe David's attitude in showing kindness to Mephibosheth? Does it seem he was under an obligation, or was he really interested in doing something good for Mephibosheth? What in the passage helps answer this question?

_____

_____

_____

3. In what ways is this story a picture of the church you've always longed for? Describe a time in your church or your own life when someone took on the concerns of another.

_____

_____

_____

4. Who is someone God may be leading you to treat as one of your own family? Is there something you can do today to show you have taken this concern on yourself?

_____

■ ■

☐ **pray** the Listening with Jesus Prayer on page 11.

☐ **Write** down something you appreciate about your church on page 40.

☐ **tell** someone what you appreciate about your church (see p. 12).

theme 1:
Work at Caring for
Your Church Family

day 6

Friday

Date _____

Read Philippians 2:1–4.

1. What reasons does Paul give for urging the Philippians to make his joy complete? According to verse 2, how were they to do that? _____

_____

2. What do verses 3–4 tell us about how we are to treat other people? Do you long for a church that practices these principles? If you practiced these principles toward others in your church, how would they respond? _____

_____

_____

3. If you went to Paul and said, "But Paul, I have this great need of my own; I can't go around helping others just now," what might he say to you?_____

_____

4. Based on this passage, what seems to be the relationship between humility and unity? How does that shape your attitude toward others in your church family?

_____

_____

5. As you've prayed the Listening with Jesus Prayer this week, how have you become more aware of your role in making the church a caring family?

_____

_____

■ ■

☐ **pray** the Listening with Jesus Prayer on page 11.

☐ **Write** down something you appreciate about your church on page 40.

☐ **read** chapter 1 in *I Like Church, But* . . . this week (see p. 21).

☐ **invite** someone to church before the Adventure is over.

27

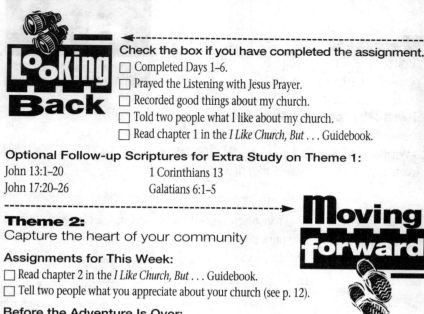

Looking Back

←--

Check the box if you have completed the assignment.
☐ Completed Days 1–6.
☐ Prayed the Listening with Jesus Prayer.
☐ Recorded good things about my church.
☐ Told two people what I like about my church.
☐ Read chapter 1 in the *I Like Church, But . . .* Guidebook.

Optional Follow-up Scriptures for Extra Study on Theme 1:

John 13:1–20   1 Corinthians 13
John 17:20–26   Galatians 6:1–5

--→

Moving forward

Theme 2:
Capture the heart of your community

Assignments for This Week:
☐ Read chapter 2 in the *I Like Church, But . . .* Guidebook.
☐ Tell two people what you appreciate about your church (see p. 12).

Before the Adventure Is Over:
☐ Invite someone to church.

Daily Assignments:
☐ Read the assigned Scripture passages and answer the questions.
☐ Pray the Listening with Jesus Prayer (see p. 11).
☐ Write down something you appreciate about your church (pp. 40–41).

An Optional Resource for Adventure Theme 2:
Conspiracy of Kindness by Steve Sjogren

This book holds a secret that has turned thousands of
people into powerful witnesses for Christ. It's a "conspiracy"
involving no-strings-attached kindness. Using unassuming
deeds of good will and humble acts of service, author Steve
Sjogren's church is showing their city the love of God. If sharing
the gospel doesn't seem to be your gift, this book will teach you
how to capture hearts in your community by showing God's love in
simple, practical ways.

*Request your copy today. Use the order form on page 80 in this journal for convenient home
delivery, or ask for this resource at your church or local Christian bookstore.*

Pray

Lord Jesus, you were so comfortable with nonreligious people that they called you a "friend of sinners." Help me to learn more about what that means.

Read

Read Acts 5:12–16.

Reflect

If your church burned down, would the people in your community really care? What if the church doors had to be permanently closed for some reason? Would anyone grieve as they passed the building?

Some churches have become adept at capturing the heart of their community. While not compromising what they believe, they are, as their Lord was, well thought of by outsiders. Today's passage states that the early Christians were highly regarded by the people, even held in a certain awe. More and more men and women were being converted, which speaks well of the impact the believers were having.

As you read these verses, do you get the feeling that the New Testament church was more community-oriented than are most churches today? If we can learn during this Adventure to cast better "shadows" as we live out our lives, it could signal the beginning of a great new day.

Apply

How does the magnetic pull of this early church compare to the impact of your congregation on the community?

_____

_____

What could your church do to capture the heart of your community?

_____

What good things happening in your church might interest your community? Who could you tell about those good things this week?

_____

Pray

Pray the Listening with Jesus Prayer.

theme 2:
Capture the Heart
of Your Community

Date _____

Read Matthew 5:13–16.

1. How is your church "salt" and "light" to the surrounding community?

_____

_____

2. A little salt and light go a long way. What are some things you personally could do to help your church be salt and light?

_____

_____

_____

3. Notice that the purpose of letting your light shine is to draw others to God. What people do you hope will see the church's light and be drawn to God? What can you do to help make that happen?

_____

_____

_____

4. Notice that salt can lose its saltiness and light can be hidden. What are specific ways you can make sure that doesn't happen during this Adventure?

_____

_____

_____

■ ■

☐ **pray** the Listening with Jesus Prayer (p. 11).

☐ **Write** down something you appreciate about your church (p. 40).

☐ **read** chapter 2 in *I Like Church, But . . .* this week (see p. 21).

theme 2:
Capture the Heart
of Your Community

day 10

Tuesday

Date _____

Read Acts 9:36–43.

1. What was the result of Peter's healing Tabitha? _____
_____

2. How did people most likely find out about this miracle? How well do you spread the news of the good things God does in your life and the life of your church?
_____
_____

3. All the widows showed Peter the clothing Tabitha had made. What might people point out to show that you are a valued member of the community (coach's whistle, baked goods for the homeless, etc.)? _____
_____
_____

4. Do you think it always takes a dramatic miracle to spread the gospel? Why or why not? What are other ways to reach out to your community and spread the Good News by word and deed? _____
_____
_____

"The hearts of our communities can be won. When Christian people build bridges, minister to needs, and unite in prayer, the power of God is released in unusual ways." Dan Lupton, *I Like Church, But . . .*, page 44

■ ■

☐ **pray** the Listening with Jesus Prayer (p. 11).

☐ **Write** down something you appreciate about your church (p. 40).

☐ **tell** someone what you appreciate about your church (see p. 12).

31

theme 2:
Capture the Heart
of Your Community

day 11

Wednesday

Date _____

Read Philippians 2:12–18.

1. According to verses 14–15, how should the world view Christians? What is necessary for Christians to "shine like stars"? _____

_____

_____

2. Paul considered his own generation "crooked and depraved." How do you think today's society compares? As things get worse in a society, does the church have more or less of a role to play? Explain. _____

_____

_____

_____

3. Do you think your community respects your church as a model of sincerity that holds out the word of life? Can you cite any specific examples?

_____

_____

4. What is a situation (maybe at work, on a committee, with your neighbors) where you could show people that you desire to represent Christ? How could you best do that?

_____

_____

5. What kinds of responses are you getting when you say good things about your church? _____

☐ **pray** the Listening with Jesus Prayer (p. 11).

☐ **Write** down something you appreciate about your church (p. 40).

☐ **read** chapter 2 in *I Like Church, But* . . . this week (see p. 21).

theme 2:
Capture the Heart
of Your Community

day 12

Read John 4:1–30, 39–42.

1. What was the end result of Jesus' asking for a drink of water from just one Samaritan woman? _____

2. How did the woman persuade the rest of the city to come and see Jesus? What does this passage show about the power of getting to know and witnessing to just one person?
_____
_____

3. What is a situation you know of where reaching out to one person ended up affecting many others? Describe what happened. _____
_____
_____

4. The disciples were surprised that Jesus was talking to this Samaritan woman. Have you ever missed an opportunity to reach out to others because you focused on "who they were" instead of on their needs? How can you prevent that from happening?
_____
_____

5. Jesus captured the heart of this woman's community. What do you long to see happen in your church that might have a significant impact on your community?
_____
_____

■ ■

☐ **pray** the Listening with Jesus Prayer (p. 11).

☐ **Write** down something you appreciate about your church (p. 40).

☐ **tell** someone what you appreciate about your church (see p. 12).

33

theme 2:
Capture the Heart
of Your Community

day 13

Friday

Date _____

Read 2 Kings 5:1–15.

1. What would have happened if the servant girl from Israel had not spoken up? What might have made this a difficult thing for her to do? _____
_____

2. Do you think Naaman would have had his spiritual needs met if he had not been drawn to Israel first because of his physical needs? What does that suggest about the value of caring for people's felt needs? _____
_____
_____

3. What are ways your church can meet the physical or material needs of unbelievers? How can that be a spiritual ministry as well? _____
_____
_____

4. Has God given you a special concern for a need you see in the community? How do you sense God would like you to respond to that need? _____
_____

"[God] is looking for people who believe that a humble demonstration of love plants a seed of eternity in the hearts of others that will blossom into faith in Christ." Steve Sjogren, *Conspiracy of Kindness,* page 11

◼ ◼

☐ **pray** the Listening with Jesus Prayer (p. 11).

☐ **Write** down something you appreciate about your church (p. 40).

☐ **read** chapter 2 in *I Like Church, But . . .* this week (see p. 21).

☐ **invite** someone to church before the Adventure is over (see p. 12).

Looking Back

Check the box if you have completed the assignment.

☐ Completed Days 7–13.
☐ Prayed the Listening with Jesus Prayer.
☐ Recorded good things about my church.
☐ Told two people what I like about my church.
☐ Read chapter 2 in *I Like Church, But . . .*

Optional Follow-up Scriptures for Extra Study on Theme 2:

John 1:43–51   Colossians 4:2–6
2 Corinthians 5:16–6:2   1 Thessalonians 2:1–13

Moving forward

Theme 3:
Welcome all people

Assignments for This Week:
☐ Read chapter 3 in *I Like Church, But . . .*
☐ Tell two people what you appreciate about your church (see p. 12).

Before the Adventure Is Over:
☐ Invite someone to church.
☐ Connect with someone outside your normal circle of friends (see p. 13).

Daily Assignments:
☐ Read the assigned Scripture passages and answer the questions.
☐ Pray the Listening with Jesus Prayer.
☐ Write down something you appreciate about your church (pp. 40–41).

Optional Resources for Adventure Theme 3:

In *Let's Get to Know Each Other*, Dr. Tony Evans provides the understanding and encouragement Christians need to help break the bonds of racial separation. Written from an African-American perspective, this compelling book offers practical suggestions to help any church welcome all people.

The *Are You My Neighbor?* Veggie Tales video is a fun way to explore Adventure Theme 3. Adults and children alike will love the original music, groundbreaking animation, and Christian values of this 30-minute treat.

Request your copies today. Use the order form on page 80 in this journal for convenient home delivery, or ask for these resources at your church or local Christian bookstore.

Days 14/15

Saturday/Sunday, Dates _____   Theme 3 runs Saturday through Friday, Days 14–20.

Pray

Lord, I love that you extend a warm welcome to all people. Help me to make sure your church follows that example.

Read

Read Acts 10:1–35.

Reflect

Making others feel welcome is not that hard. A smile can do it. A friendly greeting. A warm embrace. Conversely, it doesn't take much to let people know they're not welcome. Be condescending in the way you talk. Let your body language say, "Keep your distance." Just ignore somebody.

Jews and Gentiles knew they weren't welcome in each other's worlds. But that was changing. This is a pivotal passage in Scripture, and Peter got it right: "God does not show favoritism." Christ's church was to be inclusive, not exclusive.

Welcoming others may not be hard, but it takes work. We must work at changing attitudes, at repenting of past wrongs, at learning how to show openness, at treating others in a Christlike fashion, at recognizing the benefits of welcoming those we've kept at arm's length. Peter and Cornelius were surprised by what God had in mind. But their discovery allowed those of us who are Gentiles to be received into the family of God.

Apply

Why is it sometimes awkward to understand and welcome people from another culture?

_____

_____

What are some benefits of having a church that incorporates people from different ethnic backgrounds?

_____

_____

Pray

Pray the Listening with Jesus Prayer.

theme 3:
Welcome All People

day 16

Monday

Date _____

Read Leviticus 19:32–34 and 1 Timothy 4:12.

1. How did God expect the Israelites to treat their elders? How did he expect aliens who lived among them to be treated? _____
_____
_____

2. Have you ever been in a situation where you were the "alien"? How were you treated and how did you feel? In what ways has that experience made you respond to strangers differently? _____
_____
_____

3. Why is it sometimes difficult to understand opinions of people who are much older or much younger than you? What are the benefits of having a church that respects and listens to its younger members as well as its older members?
_____
_____
_____

4. Does age in itself make a person qualified or disqualified for a particular role in the church? What characteristics might be more important than age?
_____
_____
_____

☐ **pray** the Listening with Jesus Prayer (p. 11).

☐ **Write** down something you appreciate about your church (p. 40).

☐ **read** chapter 3 in *I Like Church, But* . . . this week.

37

Read James 2:1–9.

Date _____

1. According to James, why are we not to show favoritism?

_____

_____

2. According to this passage there are two ways to be rich. What are they? Which is more important in God's sight? _____

_____

3. Have you ever caught yourself evaluating people by the kind of clothes they wear to church? How does their appearance affect your opinion of them?

_____

_____

4. Would you be more likely to avoid a wealthy person or a poor person at church? Which action is more excusable? _____

_____

5. Do you think your church welcomes people from all economic circumstances? What can you do to avoid showing favoritism?_____

_____

"The Lord has great adventures in store for those ready to receive them. Somehow, they always seem to relate to people. So to have an adventurous life, I believe we must always be ready to welcome others." Dan Lupton, *I Like Church, But . . .* , page 66

■ ■

☐ **pray** the Listening with Jesus Prayer (p. 11).

☐ **Write** down something you appreciate about your church (p. 40).

☐ **tell** someone what you appreciate about your church.

☐ **Connect** with someone outside your circle (see p. 13).

Read Romans 14:1–12.

Date _____

1. When Paul tells the Romans not to pass judgment on "disputable matters," he means practices that are not expressly forbidden by Scripture. According to this passage, what is Paul's rationale for not judging others?

_____

_____

2. Paul uses the examples of diet and holy days as areas where believers held different convictions. What are some modern-day examples of disputable matters?

_____

_____

3. What is your response to those who have different convictions than you about disputable matters? Do you need to make any adjustments to avoid judging or looking down on your brothers and sisters in Christ?

_____

_____

_____

4. In order to welcome people who differ over the kinds of issues Paul describes, does your church need to make any changes? Explain.

_____

_____

_____

☐ **pray** the Listening with Jesus Prayer (p. 11).

☐ **Write** down something you appreciate about your church (p. 40).

☐ **read** chapter 3 in *I Like Church, But . . .* this week.

In the spaces provided, write what you appreciate about your church or church people. For more information on Action Step 2 and saying good things about your church, see page 12.

Day 1 _____

Day 2 _____

Day 3 _____

Day 4 _____

Day 5 _____

Day 6 _____

Day 7 _____

Day 8 _____

Day 9 _____

Day 10 _____

Day 11 _____

Day 12 _____

Day 13 _____

Day 14 _____

Day 15 _____

Day 16 _____

Day 17 _____

Day 18 _____

Day 19 _____

Day 20 _____

Day 21 _____

Day 22 _____

Day 23 _____

Day 24 _____

Church

Day 25 _____

Day 26 _____

Day 27 _____

Day 28 _____

Day 29 _____

Day 30 _____

Day 31 _____

Day 32 _____

Day 33 _____

Day 34 _____

Day 35 _____

Day 36 _____

Day 37 _____

Day 38 _____

Day 39 _____

Day 40 _____

Day 41 _____

Day 42 _____

Day 43 _____

Day 44 _____

Day 45 _____

Day 46 _____

Day 47 _____

Day 48 _____

Day 49 _____

Day 50 _____

Read Acts 9:19b–30.

1. Why were the Christians in Jerusalem afraid of Saul? Was their fear well founded?

_____

2. How would you respond if someone who had been killing people from your church started claiming that he or she was a Christian and wanted to join you?

_____

3. Saul eventually became the apostle Paul and greatly strengthened the church. Why might this encourage your congregation to welcome all people?

_____

_____

_____

4. What kinds of people are churches afraid of welcoming today (ex-convicts, people with AIDS, etc.)? What cautions might Christ see as appropriate or inappropriate?

_____

_____

_____

"Only by allowing the Bible to be the standard by which we judge ourselves and others can we re-experience the power necessary to be the kind of salt and light that can save a decaying society." Dr. Tony Evans, *Let's Get to Know Each Other,* page 133

☐ **Pray** the Listening with Jesus Prayer (p. 11).

☐ **Write** down something you appreciate about your church (p. 40).

☐ **tell** someone what you appreciate about your church.

☐ **Connect** with someone outside your circle (see p. 13).

Read Revelation 7:9–10.

Date _____

1. Who are the worshipers in this passage? What does this tell you about the believers you will be worshiping with in heaven?

_____

_____

2. Have you ever seen or participated in a worship service in a different cultural setting? How did it differ from your church's worship? What things were the same?

_____

_____

_____

3. Do you long for a congregation with greater diversity? What keeps that from becoming a reality?

_____

_____

_____

4. What are specific ways you can help welcome all people to your church and get a taste of what heaven will be like?

_____

_____

_____

☐ **pray** the Listening with Jesus Prayer (p. 11).

☐ **write** down something you appreciate about your church (p. 40).

☐ **read** chapter 3 in *I Like Church, But* . . . this week.

☐ **invite** someone to church before the Adventure is over.

Looking Back

Check the box if you have completed the assignment.

☐ Completed Days 14–20.
☐ Prayed the Listening with Jesus Prayer.
☐ Recorded good things about my church.
☐ Told two people what I like about my church.
☐ Read chapter 3 in *I Like Church, But . . .*
☐ Connected with someone outside my normal circle of friends.

Optional Follow-up Scriptures for Extra Study on Theme 3:
Luke 10:25–37   Ephesians 2:11–22   Galatians 3:26–29

Moving forward

Theme 4:
Empower individuals

Assignments for This Week:
☐ Read chapter 4 in *I Like Church, But . . .*
☐ Tell two people what you appreciate about your church.

Before the Adventure Is Over:
☐ Invite someone to church.
☐ Connect with someone outside your normal circle of friends (see p. 13).
☐ Help someone become all God wants him or her to be (see p. 15).

Daily Assignments:
☐ Read the assigned Scripture passages and answer the questions.
☐ Write down something you appreciate about your church (pp. 40–41).
☐ Pray the Listening with Jesus Prayer.

An Optional Resource for Adventure Theme 4:

Tales of the Restoration by David & Karen Mains

The King has broken the rule of the evil Enchanter, and the Restoration has begun! In these allegorical stories you'll meet Grandma Vigilantes, Little Child, the Girl with the Very Loud Outside Voice, and others. Each one is learning to find a special place in Bright City, to do a job that no one else can do. Hardcover with beautiful full-color illustrations, this book helps both children and adults discover how Christians can empower each other.

Request your copy today. Use the order form on page 80 in this journal for convenient home delivery, or ask for this resource at your church or local Christian bookstore.

Saturday/Sunday, Dates _____   Theme 4 runs Saturday through Friday, Days 21–27.

Pray

Lord, you recognize the potential in each of us. May I help others become all you want them to be.

Read

Read Acts 18:24–28.

Reflect

I hope you didn't read this passage too quickly. You might have missed the fact that Priscilla and Aquila did something wonderful!

Yes, they knew that the message of Apollos was not all it should be. But they also recognized the potential his skills represented for the church. And the knowledge he lacked they could easily provide. So they took the initiative and almost immediately began his tutoring. Apparently others in the church were brought into this empowering process, because Apollos traveled to Achaia with a letter of recommendation, and his gifts proved a great help to the believers there.

Most people want to become all God wants them to be. But this often requires perceptive people like Priscilla or Aquila, who see potential in others and then provide help of one kind or another. This New Testament couple had mastered a skill that also can bring great blessing to the modern church, to say nothing of the joy it will provide for all who choose to play a similar role.

Apply

What do the following references tell you about Priscilla and Aquila: Acts 18:1–3,18; 1 Corinthians 16:19; Romans 16:3–5?

_____

_____

_____

What roles (Agent, Banker, Coach—see p. 16) do you think Aquila and Priscilla played in Apollos's life? What in Scripture supports your answers?

_____

_____

Pray

Pray the Listening with Jesus Prayer.

Read Matthew 9:9–13.

Date _____

1. Tax collectors were hated by the Jews as dishonest, greedy Roman collaborators. If you had been Jesus' press secretary, how would you have defended his inviting Matthew to follow him? _____

_____

2. Do you think you would have seen Matthew's potential the way Jesus did? Why or why not? What does this passage say to you as you look for someone to empower for Action Step 4?

_____

_____

3. Who is a non-Christian "Matthew" you might begin to see as someone with kingdom potential?

_____

4. Apparently Jesus was comfortable with people who were not highly regarded by society. What reason does he give for eating with tax collectors and "sinners"?

_____

_____

"Empowering is a delightful aspect of life. It is thrilling because it looks for the potential that God sees. The cup is half-filled and moving toward overflowing." Dan Lupton, *I Like Church, But . . .*, page 90

☐ **pray** the Listening with Jesus Prayer (p. 11).

☐ **Write** down something you appreciate about your church (p. 40).

☐ **read** chapter 4 in *I Like Church, But . . .* this week.

☐ **help** someone become all God wants him or her to be (see p. 15).

Read Philemon.

Date _____

1. Under Roman law a runaway slave could be punished by any means the master thought appropriate—including death. What significance does this add to Paul's letter and decision to send Onesimus back to his owner?

_____

_____

2. In what ways could Paul's letter be seen as empowering Onesimus?

_____

_____

3. Does Onesimus seem an unlikely person to empower? As you think about empowering someone for Action Step 4, what are factors that tend to blind you to people's potential? _____

_____

_____

4. In what ways could Paul's letter be seen as empowering Philemon?

_____

_____

"For Agatha Ann had found what everyone seeks, a place to be herself, where one person at least, one very important person, cared that she could do what no one else could do." David and Karen Mains, *Tales of the Restoration*

■ ■

☐ **pray** the Listening with Jesus Prayer (p. 11).

☐ **Write** down something you appreciate about your church (p. 40).

☐ **tell** someone what you appreciate about your church.

☐ **Connect** with someone outside your circle (see p. 13).

theme 4:
Empower Individuals

Read Luke 8:1–3.

Date _____

1. In this passage, who is traveling with Jesus? How are the women helping?

_____

_____

2. In Jewish culture, women were not supposed to be taught by rabbis. What do you learn about Jesus' view of women from the fact that they were traveling with him during his public ministry? _____

_____

_____

3. Jesus empowered these women by allowing them to support his ministry and learn alongside men. What are some ways women are empowered in your church?

_____

_____

4. Are there times when churchwomen feel their gifts and talents are not fully accepted? What are some new areas or ways their gifts could be used to benefit others?

_____

_____

5. Can you think of a woman who needs to be thanked and encouraged for service to your church? What can you do to show your appreciation?

_____

_____

■ ▪ ■ ▪ ■ ▪ ■ ▪ ■ ▪ ■ ▪ ■ ▪ ■ ▪ ■ ▪ ■ ▪ ■ ▪ ■ ▪ ■

☐ **pray** the Listening with Jesus Prayer (p. 11).

☐ **Write** down something you appreciate about your church (p. 41).

☐ **read** chapter 4 in *I Like Church, But* . . . this week.

☐ **help** someone become all God wants him or her to be (see p. 15).

Read 1 Samuel 16:1–13.   Date _____

1. According to this passage, what did God look at when choosing the next king of Israel? How did that compare to Samuel's train of thought? _____

_____

2. What kinds of things fall into the category of "outward appearance"? What does God mean by looking at the heart? Which do you tend to look at more? Why?

_____

_____

_____

3. God saw David as a "diamond in the rough." How does this passage challenge the way you look at people? _____

_____

4. Where was David when Samuel invited the others to come to the sacrifice? Why do you think he was not included? What do you think was the response of Jesse and his family to David's anointing? _____

_____

_____

5. What does this account tell you about empowering the younger generation? Who is a younger person whose gifts you could help to develop?

_____

☐ **pray** the Listening with Jesus Prayer (p. 11).

☐ **Write** down something you appreciate about your church (p. 41).

☐ **tell** someone what you appreciate about your church.

☐ **Connect** with someone outside your circle (see p. 13).

theme 4:
Empower Individuals

day 27

Friday

Date _____

Read Acts 4:1–14.

1. What surprised the educated religious leaders most about Peter and John?

_____

2. What was Peter and John's occupation before they met Jesus (see Matthew 4:18–22)? Based on the Acts passage, how had being with Jesus changed their lives?

_____

_____

_____

3. Where did Peter and John get the power to heal the beggar and then preach with such boldness?_____

_____

4. In what church settings have you felt insignificant? What does this passage say to you? _____

_____

_____

_____

5. Is there anyone in your church who may feel insignificant? What would have to happen for that person to be empowered?

_____

_____

■ ■

☐ **pray** the Listening with Jesus Prayer (p. 11).

☐ **Write** down something you appreciate about your church (p. 41).

☐ **read** chapter 4 in *I Like Church, But* . . . this week.

☐ **help** someone become all God wants him or her to be (see p. 15).

50

Looking Back

Check the box if you have completed the assignment.

- ☐ Completed Days 21–27.
- ☐ Prayed the Listening with Jesus Prayer.
- ☐ Recorded good things about my church.
- ☐ Told two people what I like about my church.
- ☐ Read chapter 4 in *I Like Church, But . . .*
- ☐ Connected with someone outside my normal circle of friends.
- ☐ Helped someone become all God wants him or her to be.

Optional Follow-up Scriptures for Extra Study on Theme 4:

Luke 5:1–11   Acts 16:1–5 and 2 Timothy 1:1–7

Theme 5:
Model integrity

Moving forward

Assignments for This Week:

- ☐ Read chapter 5 in *I Like Church, But . . .*
- ☐ Tell two people what you appreciate about your church.

Before the Adventure Is Over:

- ☐ Invite someone to church.
- ☐ Connect with someone outside your normal circle of friends.
- ☐ Help someone become all God wants him or her to be.
- ☐ Get rid of personal garbage (see p. 17).

Daily Assignments:

- ☐ Read the assigned Scripture passages and answer the questions.
- ☐ Write down something you appreciate about your church (pp. 40–41).
- ☐ Pray the Listening with Jesus Prayer.

An Optional Resource for Adventure Theme 5:
Honest to God? by Bill Hybels

"Christianity is a supernatural walk with a living, dynamic, personal God. Why, then, do so many Christians live inconsistent, powerless lives?" Bill Hybels addresses this question by challenging Christians to be authentic. He outlines twelve explicit signs of inconsistent living and offers practical suggestions on what to do about them. This book should help you examine and reestablish your integrity before God and others.

Request your copy today. Use the order form on page 80 in this journal for convenient home delivery, or ask for this resource at your church or local Christian bookstore.

Saturday/Sunday, Dates _____   Theme 5 runs Saturday through Friday, Days 28–34.

Pray

Lord, you were a perfect model of integrity to a watching world. Help me, as a part of your church, to follow your example.

Read

Read Acts 5:1–11 and 20:17–18,22,32–38.

Reflect

Which of these two biblical "news stories" do you think today's press would pick up on?

The first would be sure to capture the headlines. There's action, a touch of the spectacular, and when there's sin in the church it always makes for strong reader interest.

But which account were you most drawn to?

Most Christians would prefer the second passage. This is a beautiful scene, especially when the elders of the church at Ephesus begin to cry. They realize this is undoubtedly the last time they will be with Paul, this apostle of integrity.

On a feeling level, here's how we who are part of the church want to be known—for modeling integrity in all our dealings. It shames us when the church is made to look bad in front of a watching world. More than that, we're embarrassed on Christ's behalf.

Paul was a positive example in everything he did. Ananias and Sapphira were not. What about you?

Apply

How does dishonesty among Christians impact today's church? _____

_____

How would you feel if your personal dealings were disclosed to the whole community? Do they reflect biblical or worldly standards? Explain. Are there any changes God would have you consider?

_____

_____

Pray

Pray the Listening with Jesus Prayer.

theme 5:
Model Integrity

Read Mark 11:15–17 and 2 Chronicles 29:15–20.

Date _____

1. Worshipers knew that people were being exploited by the money changers who had the full approval of the chief priests. How do you think the average person responded to Jesus' words about this being a "den of robbers" that needed to be overthrown?

_____

2. In 2 Chronicles, Hezekiah is "taking out the garbage" left by his predecessor, King Ahaz. This cleansing allowed the Israelites to begin offering sacrifices again. Predict how you think the people responded to this chance to restore their relationship with God. Then read verses 27–29 and 36.

_____

3. Do you long to be part of a congregation where spiritual garbage is not allowed to accumulate? How would that benefit a church?

_____

_____

4. Are there sins in your life that need God's cleansing? Which one might you focus on for Action Step 5 (see p. 17)?

_____

■ ■

☐ **pray** the Listening with Jesus Prayer (p. 11).

☐ **Write** down something you appreciate about your church (p. 41).

☐ **read** chapter 5 in *I Like Church, But . . .* this week.

☐ **get rid** of personal garbage (see p. 17).

Read Psalm 15.

Date _____

1. Review the qualities of the person who may dwell in God's sanctuary. Which ones mark your life? _____

_____

_____

2. Which characteristic do you have a hard time living out? Explain.

_____

3. How would a church change if all its members obeyed this psalm? Do you think the community would notice? Why or why not?

_____

_____

_____

4. Is there a situation in your life to which this psalm speaks? Consider this as you prepare to do Action Step 5 (see p. 17).

_____

_____

"Like a tree with rotting branches, the church cannot model integrity if its members or leaders don't practice what Christ taught. The way to show good character is by starting from the bottom up." Dan Lupton, *I Like Church, But . . .*, page 114

■ ■

☐ **pray** the Listening with Jesus Prayer (p. 11).

☐ **Write** down something you appreciate about your church (p. 41).

☐ **tell** someone what you appreciate about your church.

☐ **connect** with someone outside your circle.

theme 5:
Model Integrity

Read Genesis 35:1–5.

Date _____

1. After the terrible events in chapter 34, God commands Jacob to go to Bethel. What are evidences in this passage that Jacob and his family had not been living by God's standards? _____

_____

_____

2. Jacob instructs his household to cast away their idols. What kinds of "idols" are problems for God's people today?

_____

_____

3. Is there an idol in your life you need to "bury under the oak"? How does that relate to Action Step 5 (see p. 17)? _____

_____

_____

4. Jacob longed for another fresh start with God at Bethel (see Genesis 28:10–22). What would it take for you to make a fresh start with God? How might that affect your church? _____

_____

_____

_____

■ ■

☐ **pray** the Listening with Jesus Prayer (p. 11).

☐ **Write** down something you appreciate about your church (p. 41).

☐ **read** chapter 5 in *I Like Church, But . . .* this week.

☐ **get rid** of personal garbage (see p. 17).

Read Ephesians 4:22–32.

Date _____

1. In what ways have you "put off your old self"? What effect has that had in your life?

_____
_____
_____

2. Read through this passage more slowly, noticing every instruction Paul gives. Do any of these commands apply to your life today? Be specific.

_____
_____
_____

3. How would getting rid of this garbage (question 2) improve your relationship with God? How would this action improve your relationship with family, friends, or coworkers? _____

_____
_____

4. How could obeying Paul's instructions help your church become what you long for it to be? _____

_____
_____
_____

■ ■

☐ **pray** the Listening with Jesus Prayer (p. 11).

☐ **Write** down something you appreciate about your church (p. 41).

☐ **tell** someone what you appreciate about your church.

☐ **help** someone become all God wants him or her to be (see p. 15).

Read 1 Samuel 7:2–13.

Date _____

1. What were Samuel's words to Israel about returning to the Lord?

_____

_____

2. What did Samuel do after the Philistines were defeated? What was the importance of this symbol? _____

_____

3. What kind of "Ebenezer stone" would represent your renewed repentance and commitment to the Lord? (Consider carrying a cross in your pocket, framing an appropriate Scripture verse, etc.) _____

_____

4. Is it important that others in the church know about spiritual victories in your life? Why or why not? _____

_____

_____

"The dictionary defines something as 'authentic' when it 'conforms to what it is represented or claimed to be.' Authenticity means consistency—between words and actions, and between claimed values and actual priorities." Bill Hybels, *Honest to God?*, page 12

■ ■

☐ **pray** the Listening with Jesus Prayer (p. 11).

☐ **Write** down something you appreciate about your church (p. 41).

☐ **read** chapter 5 in *I Like Church, But . . .* this week.

☐ **get rid** of personal garbage (see p. 17).

☐ **invite** someone to church before the Adventure is over.

Looking Back

Check the box if you have completed the assignment.

☐ Completed Days 28–34.
☐ Prayed the Listening with Jesus Prayer.
☐ Recorded good things about my church.
☐ Told two people what I like about my church.
☐ Read chapter 5 in *I Like Church, But . . .*
☐ Connected with someone outside my normal circle of friends.
☐ Helped someone become all God wants him or her to be.
☐ Got rid of personal garbage.

Optional Follow-up Scriptures for Extra Study on Theme 5:
Acts 19:13–20   Joshua 7:1–8:1   Psalm 51

Moving forward

Theme 6:
Serve a broken world

Assignments for This Week:

☐ Read chapter 6 in *I Like Church, But . . .*
☐ Tell two people what you appreciate about your church.

Before the Adventure Is Over:

☐ Invite someone to church.   ☐ Get rid of personal garbage.
☐ Connect with someone outside your normal circle of friends.
☐ Help someone become all God wants him or her to be.

Daily Assignments:

☐ Read the assigned Scripture passages and answer the questions.
☐ Write down something you appreciate about your church (pp. 40–41).
☐ Pray the Listening with Jesus Prayer.

An Optional Resource for Adventure Theme 6:

Living in the Light of Eternity by K. P. Yohannan
Drawing from fascinating true stories and eye-opening statistics, K. P. Yohannan inspires Christians to look beyond temporary concerns and serve this broken world. He gently, urgently prompts the church: "We need to retrain our minds to interpret everything we do, everything we see, everything we spend . . . in the light of souls that are dying without Jesus."

Request your copy today. Use the order form on page 80 in this journal for convenient home delivery, or ask for this resource at your church or local Christian bookstore.

Saturday/Sunday, Dates _____   Theme 6 runs Saturday through Friday, Days 35–41.

Pray

Jesus, keep reminding me that life without you leaves a lot to be desired.

Read

Read Acts 16:6–15.

Reflect

Short-term mission trips are often eye-openers. After visiting other countries, participants usually come away with the impression that North Americans are better off than they realized.

The message of Christ and his love is so well known here. Maybe we have forgotten the great dignity it gives those who receive it.

It is an illusion to think that nations would be better off if Christians just left them alone. That's not true in terms of this life, nor of the life to come. Paul's vision of the Macedonian man was not one of someone seated comfortably, saying, "We're doing fine, but if you want to come here, feel free." This man was standing and begging Paul, "Help us"!

When is the last time you heard a cry for help? Did it seem urgent? Read that same feeling into this passage. It's a way to recapture the emotions of the scene and to remind yourself that when the church functions as it should, it reaches out to the broken of the world.

Apply

What are ways God might remind Christians today that broken people still are calling, "Come and help us"?

_____

_____

In his travel plans, Paul was open to the promptings of the Holy Spirit. How adaptable are you to the Spirit's leading toward missionary involvement?

_____

How did Lydia help facilitate the spread of the gospel? What is a tangible way you could presently be involved in a missionary outreach?

_____

Pray

Pray the Listening with Jesus Prayer.

theme 6:
Serve a Broken World

Read Matthew 25:31–46.

Date _____

1. What are the two categories of people in this passage? What defines each group?

_____

_____

2. Can you think of people you know who have the kinds of needs discussed in verses 35–36? List several people by name.

_____

_____

_____

3. How does this passage challenge you to look differently at those in need?

_____

_____

4. What is one practical way you could serve a needy person before the Adventure is over?

_____

_____

"Jesus had the wonderful ability to look at a sea of faces and see individuals needing His love. He could also look at one wounded soul and see the pain of the world in that person."
Dan Lupton, *I Like Church, But . . .*, page 129

□ **pray** the Listening with Jesus Prayer (p. 11).

□ **Write** down something you appreciate about your church (p. 41).

□ **read** chapter 6 in *I Like Church, But . . .* this week.

theme 6:
Serve a Broken World

Read Genesis 1:28–31.

Date _____

1. What was God's response to his creation? What words would you use to describe the earth as God originally fashioned it? _____

_____

2. In this passage, what are Adam and Eve instructed to do? _____

_____

_____

3. In what ways has God's creation become subjected to frustration (see Romans 8:18–21)? _____

_____

_____

4. How can Christians become better stewards of God's creation? What is one step you could take toward that end?

_____

_____

_____

5. Should the church be concerned about environmental issues? Why or why not?

_____

_____

☐ **pray** the Listening with Jesus Prayer (p. 11).

☐ **Write** down something you appreciate about your church (p. 41).

☐ **tell** someone what you appreciate about your church.

☐ **Connect** with someone outside your circle (see p. 13).

theme 6:
Serve a Broken World

Read Luke 14:12–14.

Date _____

1. According to these verses, to whom is hospitality to be shown? Why?

_____

_____

2. Does this passage affirm your lifestyle or challenge it? Explain.

_____

_____

3. Notice that these guests would have been unable to repay the gesture. Name some-one you know who would not be able to return your hospitality or kind act.

_____

4. Church people often eat together. How could you incorporate Jesus' instructions into these regular practices (i.e., invite someone for dinner or to brunch after church)?

_____

_____

5. What does this passage have to do with your church's becoming all you long for it to be? _____

_____

_____

■ ■

☐ **pray** the Listening with Jesus Prayer (p. 11).

☐ **Write** down something you appreciate about your church (p. 41).

☐ **help** someone become all God wants him or her to be (see p. 15).

theme 6:
Serve a Broken World

Read Isaiah 58:6–11.

Date _____

1. List the things Isaiah instructs the nation of Israel to do.

_____

_____

_____

2. Name someone you know who is experiencing injustice. How can you meet the challenge of this passage?

_____

_____

3. What does Isaiah say will be the results of Israel's actions?

_____

_____

_____

4. Often we think serving a broken world mainly benefits other people. What does this passage have to say about that notion? Can you think of a recent time when serving others had a positive outcome for you?

_____

_____

■ ■

☐ **pray** the Listening with Jesus Prayer (p. 11).

☐ **Write** down something you appreciate about your church (p. 41).

☐ **tell** someone what you appreciate about your church.

☐ **get rid** of personal garbage (see p. 17).

Serve a Broken World

Read James 2:14–17.

Date _____

1. In your own words, what is James's main point?

_____

_____

2. Think of a need you've heard recently. How does this passage influence you response?

_____

_____

3. Everyone has regrets about missed opportunities to help people in need. What i one situation where you wish you had a second chance to respond?

_____

4. Has praying the Listening with Jesus Prayer helped you become more responsive t people's needs? In what ways?

_____

_____

_____

"The cry of the lost world comes loud and desperate to our ears. Let us be willing to hear an respond to it." K. P. Yohannan, *Living in the Light of Eternity,* page 93

☐ **pray** the Listening with Jesus Prayer (p. 11).

☐ **Write** down something you appreciate about your church (p. 41).

☐ **read** chapter 6 in *I Like Church, But . . .* this week.

☐ **invite** someone to church before the Adventure is over.

Check the box if you have completed the assignment.

☐ Completed Days 35–41.
☐ Prayed the Listening with Jesus Prayer.
☐ Recorded good things about my church.
☐ Told two people what I like about my church.
☐ Read chapter 6 in *I Like Church, But . . .*
☐ Invited someone to church.
☐ Connected with someone outside my normal circle of friends.
☐ Helped someone become all God wants him or her to be.
☐ Got rid of personal garbage.

Optional Follow-up Scriptures for Extra Study on Theme 6:

Job 29:11–17   Luke 4:14–21   2 Corinthians 8:1–15

Moving forward

Theme 7: Encounter the living God
Theme 8: Anticipate a great future

Assignments for This Week:

☐ Read chapters 7–8 in *I Like Church, But . . .*
☐ Tell two people what you appreciate about your church.
☐ Connect with someone outside your normal circle of friends.
☐ Help someone become all God wants him or her to be.
☐ Invite someone to church.   ☐ Get rid of personal garbage.

Daily Assignments:

☐ Read the assigned Scripture passages and answer the questions.
☐ Write down something you appreciate about your church (pp. 40–41).
☐ Pray the Listening with Jesus Prayer.

An Optional Resource for Adventure Themes 7 and 8:

SoulShaping by Douglas J. Rumford

Imagine what would happen in churches if every believer learned to commune with the Lord! Dr. Douglas Rumford offers biblical tools for both unseasoned and mature disciples who want to encounter the living God. You'll often refer to this resource as you allow God to shape you.

Request your copy today. Use the order form on page 80 in this journal for convenient home delivery, or ask for this resource at your church or local Christian bookstore.

Pray

Lord, I want church to be more than mere human encounters. Help me to be aware of your presence.

Read

Read Acts 4:23–31.

Reflect

The number-one reason people go to church is to experience God. They want to encounter him in worship, sense that he speaks to them through the sermon, or meet him in a personal way during Communion.

This passage doesn't tell us where Peter and John were when they reported their meeting with the Sanhedrin. We do know that they were speaking to the gathered church. After the believers raised their voices together in prayer, the Lord revealed himself in three ways: The meeting place was shaken, the people were filled with the Holy Spirit, and they spoke the word of God boldly.

Would it be exciting to have your church sanctuary shake because of the presence of the Lord? What about knowing that everyone in attendance was being filled with the Holy Spirit and would leave the service ready to speak boldly to others about Jesus? Maybe these experiences are more than most of us are prepared for.

Certainly we all can go to church with expectancy, believing that God will be present and will make himself known to all who truly seek him.

Apply

Most Christians long for a church where the Lord's presence is experienced in the preaching, the praying, and even in the problems. When a situation over which you have little control arises in your life, how does knowing God affect your outlook?

_____

_____

How would you like to sense God's presence more fully this weekend?

_____

Pray

Pray the Listening with Jesus Prayer.

Read Mark 11:1–10.

Date _____

1. In this passage, how do the people of Jerusalem respond to their encounter with the Son of God? _____

_____

2. Do you think the people expected that this Messiah would soon be arrested, tried, and executed? Explain.

_____

_____

3. Have there been times when God's plans and your desires were far enough apart that you became confused and disappointed in him? Describe one such experience.

_____

_____

_____

4. It is because of Jesus' submission to his Father's will that he is worthy of our worship (see Philippians 2:5–11). What is a hymn or Scripture passage you can use to express your gratitude to Christ?

_____

_____

_____

■ ■

☐ **pray** the Listening with Jesus Prayer (p. 11).

☐ **Write** down something you appreciate about your church (p. 41).

☐ **invite** someone to church.

☐ **read** chapter 7 in *I Like Church, But . . .* this week.

Read Psalm 84.

Date _____

1. In your own words express the desires and longings of the psalmist. Which of these longings do you share for yourself and/or your church?

_____

_____

2. According to the psalmist, what are some of the benefits that come when one's heart is set on God? Which is most appealing to you?

_____

_____

3. Do you sense blessings similar to those described in this psalm as a result of your church experience? What is an example?

_____

_____

_____

4. How can you help make your church a place where people's longings for God are satisfied? _____

_____

"Sure, you go to church to see friends, to teach or sing, and for any number of commendable reasons. But if you didn't meet God there, you wouldn't keep it up—not for long." Dan Lupton, *I Like Church, But . . .*, page 153

■ ▪ ■ ▪ ■ ▪ ■ ▪ ■ ▪ ■ ▪ ■ ▪ ■ ▪ ■ ▪ ■ ▪ ■ ▪ ■ ▪ ■ ▪

☐ **pray** the Listening with Jesus Prayer (p. 11).

☐ **Write** down something you appreciate about your church (p. 41).

☐ **tell** someone what you appreciate about your church.

☐ **Connect** with someone outside your circle (see p. 13).

theme 7:
Encounter the Living God

day 46

Wednesday

Date _____

Read 1 Timothy 3:14–16.

1. What phrases does Paul use in these verses to describe the church?

_____

_____

2. How does Paul's perception of the church compare with the way you view your congregation? _____

_____

3. In verse 16, who is being described by these glorious words? What is one way you can prepare to meet this risen Christ when the people of God gather?

_____

_____

4. What keeps people from encountering the living God in church? What can you do to break through any of these barriers?

_____

_____

_____

"God is always with us. But we must learn how to heighten our own awareness of his presence and his work in and around us. Then we can actually behave and believe like people who have God with them every moment." Douglas J. Rumford, *SoulShaping*

■ ■

☐ **pray** the Listening with Jesus Prayer (p. 11).

☐ **Write** down something you appreciate about your church (p. 41).

☐ **read** chapter 7 in *I Like Church, But . . .*

☐ **help** someone become all God wants him or her to be (see p. 15).

Day 47   Introduction to Theme 8: Anticipate a Great Future

Thursday, Date _____   Theme 8 runs Thursday through Sunday, Days 47–50.

Pray

Lord Jesus, because we know who you are, we look to the future with confidence and joy.

Read

Read Matthew 16:13–21.

Reflect

Fans are more supportive of winning teams than of losing ones. Investors want success stories, not failures. And Jesus' disciples needed assurance that his church would be victorious.

To emphasize this point, our Lord took the disciples to Caesarea Philippi. Herod the Great had built a temple there to Augustus Caesar. One of Herod's sons, Philip the tetrarch, renamed the city so that it became known as Philip's Caesarea to distinguish it from the port city of Caesarea on the Mediterranean. In this place where numerous gods were worshiped, including the powerful Roman emperor, our Lord acknowledged Peter's affirmation that he indeed was the Son of God.

From that point on, Jesus began speaking freely about his death. The Anointed One of God would suffer many things. But he would rise again, and his church would storm the very gates of Hades.

We are on the winning team. All who invest their lives in Christ can anticipate a great future. We confidently rejoice even now, knowing that his church ultimately will be victorious.

Apply

Do you ever feel frustrated when your longings for the church are not immediately realized? What perspective does this passage give on the future of the church as it battles the powers of evil? _____

_____

As you approach the end of this Adventure, how are you stronger in the Lord than you were at the beginning?_____

_____

Pray

Pray the Listening with Jesus Prayer.

theme 8:
Anticipate a Great Future

Read Psalm 22.

Date _____

1. Jesus quoted from this psalm on the Cross (see Matthew 27:46). Which verses anticipate the events of Good Friday?

_____

_____

_____

2. How does this psalm help you picture Christ's suffering more vividly? Which images especially stand out for you?

_____

_____

3. At the end of the psalm, what things does the author, David, anticipate?

_____

_____

_____

4. What future benefits of Christ's death and resurrection do you long for most? Take time now to list some of them as you give thanks for what lies ahead.

_____

_____

■ ■

☐ **pray** the Listening with Jesus Prayer (p. 11).

☐ **Write** down something you appreciate about your church (p. 41).

☐ **tell** someone what you appreciate about your church.

☐ **get rid** of personal garbage (see p. 17).

theme 8:
Anticipate a Great Future

day 49

Saturday

Read 1 Peter 1:3–9.

Date _____

1. Peter is writing to believers who were being persecuted for their faith. What explanation does he give for their griefs and trials?

_____

_____

2. Peter promises a future unlike the present. How does he describe it, and what emotions does it produce?

_____

_____

3. What griefs or trials are you or others in your church experiencing? What encouragement do you draw from this passage?

_____

_____

_____

4. What is one way this Adventure has rekindled your hope for the church?

_____

_____

"The prospects for the church today are brightest when God's people daily prepare themselves for the Lord's return by confession of sin and a longing to be holy." Dan Lupton, *I Like Church, But . . .*, page 189

■ ■

☐ **pray** the Listening with Jesus Prayer (p. 11).

☐ **Write** down something you appreciate about your church (p. 41).

☐ **read** chapter 8 in *I Like Church, But . . .*

☐ **invite** someone to church.

theme 8:
Anticipate a Great Future

Read Acts 9:1–19.

Date _____

1. What was Saul's mission before he met Jesus, the risen Lord? How did this encounter change his life? _____

_____

_____

2. Ananias probably found it hard to believe that Paul had become a Christian. Is there a situation in your life or the life of your church that seems beyond the power of God? What insights do you gain from this account?

_____

_____

3. Do you long for a church that expects great things from God? How can you personally demonstrate that kind of attitude? _____

_____

_____

4. What is a lesson you've learned during this Adventure? What habits do you sense God wants you to continue as a part of the church you've always longed for?

_____

_____

_____

■ ■

☐ **pray** the Listening with Jesus Prayer (p. 11).

☐ **Write** down something you appreciate about your church (p. 41).
Does your chart have 50 entries?

☐ **Complete** page 74 to bring closure to your Adventure.

☐ **Share** your Adventure experience with The Chapel Ministries (and receive a free book). See page 77.

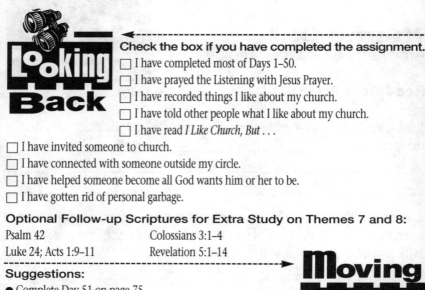

Check the box if you have completed the assignment.

☐ I have completed most of Days 1–50.

☐ I have prayed the Listening with Jesus Prayer.

☐ I have recorded things I like about my church.

☐ I have told other people what I like about my church.

☐ I have read *I Like Church, But . . .*

☐ I have invited someone to church.

☐ I have connected with someone outside my circle.

☐ I have helped someone become all God wants him or her to be.

☐ I have gotten rid of personal garbage.

Optional Follow-up Scriptures for Extra Study on Themes 7 and 8:

Psalm 42   Colossians 3:1–4

Luke 24; Acts 1:9–11   Revelation 5:1–14

Suggestions:

● Complete Day 51 on page 75.

● Continue to study Scripture and pray daily.

● Continue to say good things about your church.

● Continue to connect with people outside your normal circle of friends.

● Continue to help people become all God wants them to be.

● Continue to get rid of personal garbage regularly.

● Look at pages 76–80 for other Adventure follow-up ideas.

Your Adventure Doesn't Have to End!

Has this 50-Day Spiritual Adventure moved you closer to God, helped you develop healthy spiritual habits, or refreshed your spiritual life? Then these other Adventures by The Chapel Ministries with enable you to keep growing spiritually in the weeks to come. You can continue to Adventure all year long by ordering any one of these available 50-Day Spiritual Adventures:

● What to Do When You Don't Know What to Do

● Facing Down Our Fears

● Daring to Dream Again

● Survival Skills for Changing Times

For more information on our 50-Day Spiritual
Adventures, see page 79.

Day 51

Monday, Date _____

Pray

Lord Jesus, I want our church to be so conscious of your presence that it won't make any difference whether you are there bodily or in Spirit.

Read

Can you recall sitting in a meeting at church and wishing it didn't have to last so long? Maybe it was a board or committee meeting, and you were hoping it would finish earlier than usual.

NOW READ LUKE 24:33–53.

Reflect

What would happen if Christ suddenly appeared at a church gathering as he did in this passage? What an immense difference it would make if he took a half hour or so to unfold what the Scriptures have to say about him. What a challenge to hear him say we were his witnesses to the world (Acts 1). What an incredible promise—that we could be "clothed with power from on high."

In times of revival the presence of the Lord is felt powerfully throughout the church. Conversely, during periods of spiritual lethargy the business of the church is carried on as though Jesus were far away.

The church we long for is one that functions in the reality of the presence of the ascended Christ. It offers its heartfelt praise to the One who sits at the right hand of his Father. Its members wear the armor of God and walk in his Spirit. This is the kind of church that even today knows Christ's blessings, and because of that it is characterized by great joy.

Apply

If the risen Christ appeared at a gathering of your church, what scripture might he unfold to encourage or challenge your congregation? In what areas do you or your church need to be clothed with power from on high?

Pray

Lord, clothe us with your power from on high.

To order Discovery *or other age-graded Scripture Union devotional resources, see the order form on page 76.*

You've Finished the Adventure—Now What?

It's time to make a lifestyle out of growing spiritually!

Healthy spiritual habits like daily Scripture reading and prayer have been a part of your life for the past 50 days. Don't let them stop now!

Consider using a Scripture Union devotional guide to maintain the disciplines you've practiced throughout the Adventure. You can benefit from these devotionals all year round. In fact, you've already used the Scripture Union format with the theme introduction pages in this journal.

There are Scripture Union devotionals for adults, teens, and children. *Quest* is available for children ages 7–10. *One to One* is for youth ages 11–14. *Discovery* is a personal application guide for mature young people and adults, and *Encounter with God* is an advanced Bible study guide. So everyone can take up the challenge of making healthy spiritual habits last all year long!

See Preview Option Below

You may order Scripture Union devotionals for yourself, your family, or for friends by calling The Chapel Ministries at 1-800-224-2735 or by filling out the order form below and mailing it with your check.

☐ Yes! I would like to order an annual subscription. (Check all that apply.)

☐ OR: Please send me preview copies for $1.00 each. (Check your choices—one copy per title.)

	Price	Qty	Total Amt
☐ Discovery (adult application)	$20.00		
☐ Encounter with God (adult study)	$20.00		
☐ One to One (ages 11–14)	$20.00		
☐ Quest (ages 7–10)	$20.00		
☐ Preview copies	$1.00/ea		
	Grand Total Enclosed		

Please provide the information below:

Your Name _____

Address _____

City _____ State/Prov _____ Zip/Code _____

Phone (____) _____

Make checks payable to The Chapel Ministries.

Send this order form to:
The Chapel Ministries, Box 30, Wheaton, IL 60189-0030.
Or call 1-800-224-2735 (in Canada 1-800-461-4114) for credit card orders.

All devotionals will be sent every three months for one year.   SU697

The Chapel Ministries Wants to Hear from You!

Our feedback helps us evaluate the effectiveness of the Spiritual Adventure. Please fill out this comment form and tell us what God did in your life, your church, or your small group during this 50-day journey. In return for your feedback, we'd like to say thanks by sending you one of the free resources shown on the next page. Simply choose the one you'd like to receive!

Tell us a story of how this Adventure has changed your life or the life of your church or small group.

_____

_____

_____

_____

_____

_____

_____

_____

_____

_____

How can we improve the 50-Day Adventure for you?

_____

_____

_____

_____

How were you involved in the 50-Day Adventure? (Check all that apply.)

- [ ] Individual
- [ ] Family
- [ ] Sunday school class
- [ ] Entire church
- [ ] Small group
- [ ] Other _____

Did you tune in to any of the Adventure programs on the "You Need to Know" television program?　　[ ] Yes　　[ ] No

For your FREE "thank you" gift, turn to the next page!

Choose your free gift!

- ☐ *Open Heart—Open Home* by Karen Burton Mains
- ☐ *Back to Your Spiritual Future: Recapturing "First Love" Intensity in Your Relationship with Christ* by Steve Bell
- ☐ *Carry Me: Discoveries on the Journey from Fear into God's Arms* by Christine Wyrtzen
- ☐ *Scared to Life: Awakening the Courage of Faith in an Age of Fear* by Douglas J. Rumford

Fill out the information below:

Name _____

Address _____

City _____ State/Prov _____ Zip/Code _____

Church Name and City _____

TV station on which you watch "You Need to Know" _____

Periodically we include Adventure testimonies in our newsletters and mailings. May we contact you for more information about your story? _____

Phone (_____) _____

Mail this comment form to:
   The Chapel Ministries, Box 30, Wheaton, IL 60189-0030
   In Canada: Box 2000, Waterdown, ON L0R 2H0

Or e-mail us your comments at: T50DSA@aol.com   FBC97

Continue the Adventure All Year Long!

this Adventure has helped you develop healthy spiritual habits,
en why not use one of our other 50-Day Adventures:

hat to Do When You Don't Know What to Do
usting Christ When Life Gets Confusing

creasingly our society is characterized by confusion. But life can be lived
th perspective and direction. This 50-Day Spiritual Adventure will help
u find practical ways to trust Christ when life gets confusing.

hat to Do When You Don't Know What to Do Adult Journal and
hen Life Becomes a Maze necessary book—$12 for both

acing Down Our Fears
nding Courage When Anxiety Grips the Heart

e there areas in your life where you feel afraid? We're all afraid of some-
ing, but don't give up just yet! In this 50-Day Spiritual Adventure you'll find
actical and biblical suggestions for finding courage and overcoming fear.

cing Down Our Fears Adult Journal and
w to Fear God Without Being Afraid of Him necessary book—$12 for both

aring to Dream Again
reaking Through Barriers That Hold Us Back

od has big dreams for us, but sometimes we lose sight of his great
ans. Through this 50-Day Spiritual Adventure you'll find solutions
problems that can keep you from living God's dreams.

aring to Dream Again Adult Journal and
w to Be a World Class Christian necessary book—$12 for both

urvival Skills for Changing Times
urposeful Christian Living in the '90s

Christians we don't need to be overcome by the complexities of
e in the '90s. Through this 50-Day Spiritual Adventure, you'll
xplore specific skills found in Scripture that will help you survive—
d thrive—in our culture today.

urvival Skills Adult Journal and
etting Beyond "How Are You" necessary book—$12 for both

equest your copies of these Chapel Ministries resources today. Use the order form on page 80
this journal for convenient home delivery, or ask for them at your church or local Christian
ookstore.

The Chapel Ministries Resources Order Form

Item	Title	Retail	Qty	Total
2710	Adult Journal	6.00		
2760	Spanish Adult Journal	6.00		
2720	Student Journal	6.00		
2730	Children's Journal	6.00		
2740	Critter County Activity Book	6.00		
450X	Critter County Scripture Memory Tape	6.00		
1809	*I Like Church, But . . .* Guidebook	6.00		
450Y	*I Like Church, But . . .* Audio Guidebook	12.00		
7796	Make It Happen Scripture Pack	1.00		
1810	Conspiracy of Kindness	11.00		
1811	Let's Get to Know Each Other	11.00		
8425	Veggie Tales: Are You My Neighbor?	15.00		
1812	Tales of the Restoration	19.00		
1813	Honest to God	13.00		
1814	Living in the Light of Eternity	12.00		
1815	SoulShaping	11.00		
5720	What to Do Adult Journal and book	12.00		
5689	Facing Down Our Fears Adult Journal and book	12.00		
5690	Daring to Dream Again Adult Journal and book	12.00		
5691	Survival Skills Adult Journal and book	12.00		

Subtotal _____

Add 10% for UPS shipping/handling ($4.00 minimum) _____

Canadian or Illinois residents add 7% GST/sales tax _____

Total (subtotal + shipping + tax) _____

Here's my donation to help support the work of The Chapel Ministries _____

TOTAL AMOUNT ENCLOSED _____

Ship my order to:

Name _____

Street Address* _____ City _____

State/Prov _____ Zip/Code _____ Phone (___) _____

*(Note: UPS will not deliver to a PO box.)

I watch "You Need to Know" on television station _____

Mail this order form with your check made payable to:
    The Chapel Ministries, Box 30, Wheaton, IL 60189-0030
    In Canada: Box 2000, Waterdown, ON L0R 2H0

For U.S. VISA, MasterCard, and Discover card orders call 1-800-224-2735.
In Canada call 1-800-461-4114.